THE DRAGON IN THE LIGHTHOUSE

BY

MICHAEL SHELTON

Paperback ISBN: 978-1-960853-56-1

eBook ISBN: 978-1-960853-57-8

Liberation's Publishing – Columbus, MS

THE DRAGON IN THE LIGHTHOUSE

TABLE OF CONTENTS

5

MICHAEL SHELTON

THE CAGE

The subtle thief of time will turn
like butter in an ancient churn

But slowly does it pass by me,
Then goes with little sympathy.

"Delight in its disordered" wake
Will take not one hand up, nor shake,

But leaves for its own selfish sake,
Then starts a fire
Nightmare's Wake!

That subtle thief has robbed me blind
of youthful journey to unwind

The mainspring waiting to explode
as hair turned silver and shoulders bowed

Delighting in disordered age
Magnifying every word and page
And leaving me bleeding in my cage

A TRIBUTE TO LOVE MISSPOKEN

"If you live with me, I'll be your mael."
read Chris and Walter the bedtime tales

And take you down upon the sea
and make you there remember me!

If you believe this color the lines
inside or out, we'll still be fine

I'll quote Marlowe by line and verse
and Sir Raleigh, Elizabeth's Curse

Which one was time could not stand still
by me through work and perfect will;

I could not be one nor the other
Don't want to be and wouldn't bother

I fish for knowledge and pure adventure
When upon the ocean blue
The ladies fair must wait their turn
As I wait here for you.

+

ALEX'S SMILE

Every time I saw that lovely smile
It made that moment a little brighter
And when she wasn't at the park
my heart was a little bit lighter

For I knew that God was holding her hand
The hand of His ultimate fighter
While she made other's lives heavenly
and her own wings a little bit wider

She fought as hard as any warrior
But she never fought alone
Her tea, her foes, her family
Were as solid as a stone

Behind her each and every day
A field, in class, at church, at home
She's a beautiful angel for the Lord
Whose smile now rivals the dawn!

EPITAPH

I will be missed as one of us
From birth to death, from dust to dust

The poet, writer, teacher, that's me,
Now writing on a cloud... eternally!"

I pray that you remember me well
And that clouds are only steam in hell!

Neither is ink black as Satan's soul
Or the ink that penned the Bible's goal,

The goal that binds us for ever to GOD,
Vis discipline that doesn't exclude the rod

Like my parents did so lovingly,
then explain their act of love to me!

I can't wait to join them in laughter and tears
on my final day despite all my fears!

ANABEL'S SONG

Storms beat upon the walls below
A symphony created by waves and gales
Echoing thunder and lightning's show
Dancing across the eternal mael!

She could not see the guiding light
Emanating from the hidden shore
That disappeared into the waning night
Behind the Ravens (pallid?) door!

While storms did little to sate heartache
Of lonely tars yearning for mate

Who he upon this stormy shore
Singing siren's songs from day to yore
Asking love but nothing more
From words comprising ancient lore

MICHAEL SHELTON

THE MONSTER'S PLIGHT

When stopping by a snowy wood
Be careful of the frosty good

That comforts, lures, or even kills
The likes of so many Jacks and Jills

Be careful of confrontations like
Hansel and Gretal's witching plight
Trolls beneath the bridge at night
And warts on ogre's noses, a fright!

Be careful of the ocean's tide
Where tales were told of Triton's bride
Where mermaids have a dolphin's stride
And sailors told tales but never lied

Then take the yellow brick road to where
The werewolves howl through all that hair
Vampires in daylight must wouldn't dare
And the monster under the bed's a bear!

THE BARNYARD FAMILIES

That rooster crowed at every hour
The hen's clucked a mother's tune
The chick peep-peeped a song so sour
That I evoked a spell with Celtic rune

The barnyard filled with crimson flood
To feed the starving infant there
A dry comb of oats and blood
Fed to human and beast of Vanity Fair!

The lambs lay quiet in the darkening night
While the stars and the moon lay silent
The rams kept watch in absence of light
O'er the ewes and the lambs so pliant!

The lows of the cattle and the nays of mares
Were muted by stacks and bales of hay
While the wild beast lay in dens and lairs
And celestial crisscrossed the Milky Way!

THINGS I LOVE

I'm making a list of my favorite things
Like when Christmas comes, and snowbirds sing

Ringing like carols from the streets below
Or crunching like ice over new fallen snow!

Scottish kilts vin Celtic lass played on the radio
Beautiful tunes and beautiful ladies everyone a glow

A roaring fire dances, crackles, and glows
Keeps me warm and cozy as it comes and goes

While a lighthouse scans an angry sea
To save the frightened far in me

The smell of yeast bread and coffee brewing
Chess pies, sweet meats, our new kitten mewing!

They combine to create the most wonderful day
Like falling from the loft in a barn of fresh hay

EUROPE

My thoughts of late have been of fuzzy dreams
Warming my core with French latte creams

Dreams of the Danube and Alpine tors
Invade the dreams through dozens of doors

The City of Lights mythologies and Gaul
Start a road of conquest to empirical halls

A poet displaced in a hundred-year show
Could be no more romantic than E.A. Poe

Yet no more loving that Yeats to Gonne,
Nor more fulfilling than Ovid and Donne,

Be it sculpted or part of historical lore
We must row together with a common oar

EDUCATION

There are ladies and gentlemen
Old and young
Teaching and learning from a well that has sprung

In the minds and hearts and hopeful souls
That welcome the spirits who were lost in the cold

And warmed them in soft glowing embers
On each twenty-fifth day of each December

For learning isn't homework and behaving in school
The Ten Commandments nor the Golden Rule

A book of etiquette or the Serenity Prayers
It's control of self that needs so much care!

Whether high school students with no sense at all
Or new college students who have answered the call
These kids surrounding me don't respect the fall
That will inevitably come their way
on some dark, stormy, foreboding day

When some old man takes social security away
to pay for the old man's being deaf or blind
Or a young maid's urgent need to unwind
with a little Mary Jane, Juul or Time

DIVORCE, DEATH, FREEDOM AND WAR

The price of freedom lay mum beneath
those fifty stars and thirteen stripes
at the bottom of a glass of bourbon
Two years cling to ice cubes,
symbolic of the twenty years I'd spent alone

Blood ran down his chest
Form the hole in his temple
Where it hurt the most, a veteran's ghost
While one of my four crept through the door
On the back of my loneliness

Mom finally succumbed to an aneurism,
Dad a heart attack, sis to ovarian cancer.
ON TV hundreds died in the news
Protests, wars, and terrorism
All fought in the name of freedom
Of self or religion of speech
No one knowing just where to go!

BEGGIN THE WEATHER?

Creeping squirrels with nuts in their mouths
are scampering access my roof
Dropping leaves and dropping and hulls,
while they make their ways as proof

That autumn has arrived a little early
with its yellows, oranges, and reds
Its mossy greens winter browns
all making room in their beds

For the gentle touch of autumn's ring
And its comfort that's soon to follow
October blues November thanks
through valley over hill and hollow

But the weather of the late is too darned hot
To enjoy un-air conditioned
So, I stay inside just out of reach
And rely on Mother Nature's discretion

SEASONS OF THE COUNTRY

Falling waters and rising smoke
Could ask no better for country folk!

Then rising spirits and falling snow
as I take the opportunity to grow.

But I'm only ten and maybe a half...
going to the backyard to take a bath

In falling water provided by the rain
That is sunshine warmed to lessen pain!

I see and smell more rising smoke
that cooks my meals and heats my home...

Then into the garden for a pear or two
And the backyard again for a plum to chew

MICHAEL SHELTON

EQUINOX IN THE FALL

The autumn equinox
September 23rd, a Monday box
To an Aquarian this is romantic enough
without the advent of sexual love
The colors of orange, yellow, brown, and red,
cover the butterfly wings and head
As they do in the trees and on the ground
Fluttering loudly without a sound!

MY SEASON

This is a beautiful day of gray and green
somewhere between autumn and a winter scene

It's cool and comfortable with just a slight breeze
no sun, no rain as it blows through the trees

There are spider plants raising their little red heads
And an owl hoot-hooting from its daytime bed

I am fighting the urge to decorate and then
Go Christmas shopping with my best friend!

I set up Pandora with Holiday tunes
after listening to Celtic ladies and Enya croon

I'm watching elves, St. Nick and helpers galore
ushering in my season, one of many more!

I wrote a poem as always for the holiday season,
but I've never left out goods one reason

The breath of His son mid shepherd and sheep
While the babe in the manger lay fast asleep

And Mary and Joseph, with an angelic choir
spent the nativity with but on desire!

Then I'd sit on my deck as I do every year
while I hum "White Christmas" then many a year

And wish that my family could all gather round
to join in the thanks for what we have found

A savior born up on this day long ago
without a single tear or a flake of snow!

A BETTER HOUR

I'm stuck between a nap in my hammock
And putting up my Christmas tree
For my mood is one of jolly slumber
Butter rum and Irish cream!

Christmas never seems to come fast enough
And always leaves too soon
With a little Thanksgiving and Halloween
To slow the pace of the moon!

This year, I've begged for ice and snow
To decorate my neighborhood
With a sled on the hill in my front yard
And a return to my childhood!

The chimes in the old chapel tower
Fill the air each day with song
Taking me back to a better hour
Where I will always belong!

WORDS AND PECANS

Pecans make wonderful daily gifts
to neighbors and family and friends
And returns to me in candy and pieces
so much more I receive than send

I surround myself as much as I can
with athletic and intelligence
Especially this cooling time of year
of Christmas joy and frankincense

For twenty-five years I've taught them
and loved them long and well
With stories poems words of the world
and encouraged their own words to tell

So, at this time of year with a pie or two
I'm reminded of but ask nothing more
Then a visit, pralines, and pecan pie
and a gentle knock at my door!

THE SCENT OF A WOMAN

I cannot describe how it makes me feel
Except with a tear or two
A romantic scene or loving idea
that isn't wrong or taboo

It comes and goes without regret
This scene of loving woe
For I am used to it by now
no matter when or where I go

This scent of a woman I cannot have
will haunt me night and day
I can only possess her in my dreams
when she gives me leave to say

With vows that once I uttered clear
No twice or thrice or even four
It occurs to me that I was sincere
not once but many, many more!

A STUDY IN SIMILE

The bumblebee stepped and stared at me
hovering like a heli-jet!
Like it somehow held and cared for me
like a baby does with it's wet

It came like a stranger up the stairs
One foot one step at a time
As slow as old men or sleeping bears
awaiting the waking bell to chime

I turned its back like it feared me less
Then it had just seconds ago
O'er the rail into spring air blessed
like easter before the last snow

Then it turned and fired an angry look
challenging me to action
So, I grabbed my swatter and tome sized book
as the next great coming attraction!

THE BUMBLEBEE DIN

A single bumblebee floating on air
Then darted to and fro
wound her way into a maypole dance
Round and round she would go!

Creating patterns to an Irish jig
Or the steps of Scottish country folk
I walked alongside her upon the air
With bare feet awaiting an evening soak

The grass was green and cool and sweet
While I harkened to Celtic Ladies Wails
and trod the clover in counts of three
and gathered the lucky ones in my sails

The borders of the yard all trimmed in red
With the green and white filled in
Welcome the spring with crickets' songs
And a wonderful, humming bumble bee din!

THE NEWS

Since I've been staying here at home
I've had good news and that alone

I guess I only needed the time
To do crosswords and create rhyme

I've said a thoughtful prayer or tow
To help me out as well as you!

I've created brand new poetry and fiction,
And boned upon my grammar and diction!

I've rewatched great games from M. S. U.
And will recall hundreds before I'm through

I've found how great my friends truly are
And that I do not really miss my car!!

But most of all I've regained my faith
And don't really fear any monstrous wraith!

DON'T GIVE ME NO BAD NEWS

Got tired of only bad news and games!
I've gained five pounds with grilling flames!

I go for the news at the convenient store
But four quarters first at Campus Book Store.

That's all I do each and every day
Until someone finds another way

To Pass the time by stirring the pot!
Until that time, that's all I've got!

THE WOOD

Watch out for witches of the wood;
The hag is assuredly up to no good!

For makes a great place for her to hide,
Darkness has spread the wood far and wide!

The moss is a Bonney Irish shade of green
As emerald as any I've ever seen.

Droplets of water are of equal hue,
Reflecting the woods on evening dew.

Her visage and clothing are lost in the night
She's still as a shadow on its moonless flight.

She waits there behind the mossy oak tree;
Just out of sight of the witch stands me!

In my Tartan kilt with my Celtic rune,
I await the witch by the light of no moon!

JOHN WAYNE AND JESUS CHRIST

I'm listening to the thunder
and the pouring rain
Watching John Wayne
movies in black and white

The sky is graying with disdain and refrain,
creating a fearsome scene of daylight
hours and the dead of night.

There seems to be a lull as in the
eye of the storm, bringing calm
like that as Jesus succumbed!

But somehow, I feel oh so safe and
warm lying in the bosom of the Lord
as Christ lay peacefully in his tomb!

TWIX A VIRUS AND A HARD PLACE

I'm stuck between a rock and
the hardest place I could find
Tornados coming from the south
and a virus keeping me confined.

I prefer to stay here at home
in myself imposed quarantine
than to chance the wrath of nature
with me stuck in between.

This easter morn might come and go
with no one seated on the pew,
but God will know where each heart lies
whether many or just a few!

SONG OF SPRING

I had a conversation with a bumblebee;
She hovered round my nose as she talked to me!

I oiled the squeak in my backyard swing,
That I might not disturb a living thing.

Including her who spoke with a buzz
what will be, what is, and assuredly was!

A butterfly of colorful orange and black
and another with a painting upon its back.

Came flitting by seeking nectar sweet
and sat upon a petal at my feet.

The bumblebee hung and buzzed in the air
as the colors of spring grew everywhere.

And the wind whispered low, "come softly to me"
on the wings of an angel thru cloud and tree

Come to me in the song of the mockingbird's
whisper in my ear each and every word

Come to Mississippi with a song in your heart
And paint me a masterpiece of loving art
Sing to the mockingbird and bumblebee
 a song from the heart; make it just for me

WHAT I LIKE AND LOVE

I like a hawk, but love an owl
for the wisdom that it brings;
I like the romance of the rain
but love the rolling thunder.

I like a lonely forsaken howl,
and mama bird's song she sings;
I love a long and shady lane
mother nature in all her wonder.

I love to go out at night and prowl
or stay in with knightly queens and kings;
I like to eat strips of sugarcane
on top of the porch or under

I love to hear my stomach growl,
those jingle bells as they ring
My nose against a winter windowpane
and a good night's winder's slumber

I love my Bible; Luke 2:10
Good tidings, great joy shall be all men

Said the angel of the Lord to the faithful there
on that Holy Night in the Silence of the air

In the presence of the shepherd in a lowly manger
while all of the time in grave mortal danger

Protected by the angels and wise magic kings

while the host of angels sang and spread their wings
I love the words of the nativity scene

and the joy and peace it all brings;

And I love when my students turn to paper, and pen
look up at me halfway finished and grin

"We did it Mr. S and we did it like you.
Teach us more Mr. S before you are through."

SINNING OUR WAY TO HELL

In the desert we're deciding just who we should fight;
The television screen is filled with plight.

Outside it is pouring a romantic Southern Shower
While I sip... and pray that I have enough power

To withstand the onslaught of earth and heaven
The storms of now and Revelation's dire seven!

Be we need to reprint those seven deadly woes
For the skin and greed this generation shows!

PERSONAL GARDEN

I decided the morning to change my direction,
And not to be part of this modern insurrection,

But to create my own in this time and place
With a snap of my fingers and smile on my face.

I will not be a martyr, a king, nor a judge.
I will hold my temper, but never a grudge.

I won't look to the world for guidance and care
When my Bible lies close for me to share

The words that have echoed through my mind
Each time I've needed help or just a sign

To comfort my woes and ease my pain
Whether tomorrow brings me sunshine or rain.

The direction I choose will become of my own
Via what has made me and seed I've sown

MEMORIAL DAY

It was not a fog I felt in the air
It was only a misty rain
The wind blew it softly through my hair
And curled it into a chain

The smoke from a nearby barbecue
Urged me to join its holiday
But the recent telling of a few
Kept my friends to the robin and jay

The graveyard became a lonely place
Where I could celebrate
With the misty rain upon my face
That was bowed to meet its fate

Then I whispered softly o'er the grave
"Thank You that I am free!"
Thank you that you chose me to save
As we celebrate liberty!

IT'S THAT KIND OF WEATHER

Somehow today it's seventy-six degrees
With little humidity and temperate breeze

I am sitting a deck black ink in hand
Drying quickly beneath a ceiling fan

Writing such verses as top please the bards
Which may not be from pen, but still in the cards

I'm listening to Enya, New Age Rock-N-Rollers
Who is of Irish descent as my derby bowler.

The clouds seem to be a thin sheet of gray,
Going south to north on this last Thursday!

It'll likely go elsewhere tomorrow
Spreading its woe, danger and sorrow.

But for today, the sun shines bright
While I wait new words to write!

A STATE OF DAMN NATION

Some folks want to blame Donald
Some say it's McDonald Ronald!

Some say it's just black and white;
Some say evil happens only at night.

Some say these words; protect and serve,
Are displayed there to strike a nerve.

Some say we're all in this together,
Just standing by for stormy weather

Some say one dying is way too many
That healing comes when there aren't any!

Some wait impatiently for November,
Metaphorically waiting to dismember

The heads of those who disagree
Who yesterday were good friends to me!

AN EDENISTIC UTOPIA

I have this place almost at peace
Just one or two wrinkles I have to crease,
Just a couple of squeaks I have to grease
To put my home at perfect peace.

I have a cup of coffee well in hand!
Celtic ladies and Enya have formed a band;
Memories spread slowly across the land,
While old sweet Joes is close at hand.

Dean Koontz is taking me to other worlds!
The wind is blowing around my curls
The meeting today is for guys, not girls,
Who might have taken me to other worlds.

Today is a respite buried deep in the wood,
Or atop a mountain If Only I could
On a field of play where I'd no good
But in Sherwood Forest with Robin Hood.

THE LOOK ON HER FACE

The laughing visage of the man in the moon
And the crying eyes of the Ides of June
Are welcomed by the ways of the nocturn stars
Floating through the sky and neighborhood wars

The horrors that arise at the witching hour
Of the love of Jesus in a winter snow shower
Are as cold to one another as a Tell-Tale Heart
Beating slower and louder till they're torn apart!

But the heart and the eyes are windows to the soul;
As my relationship with Edgar Allen Poe,
Or his to the beautiful Annabel Lee
Who he's with her kinsmen and waits to be free

Yet another of the angels waiting high upon in the air
Looking down upon Earth and hoping to share
A Heavenly visage that soon would be there
Paying celestial cost with a hellish fare!

A DRINK, A JOURNEY AND A LINE OR TWO

I've always believed that If I drink
I'll be a scotch on the rock's kind of guy
If I own a barque, I'll keep my own log
And write every single line with a sigh

Should I stay aground I'll ride the rails
As brandy will be my drink of choice,
And I'd sing my words or write them
With a quiet unassuming voice!

For dinner I'll ride my imagination
With a medicinal goblet of red wine
Whether I dine with kings and wizards
Or the occupants of the lowly sties.

Sweet Dreams is tea on my back porch,
And it tastes just like it sounds
A poetic journey behind closed tired eyes
Mid pages of elves and the Baskerville hounds.

PLACES IN MY BACKYARD

I bought a set of Michelin tires then
remembered I'd given away my car!
That was ok because I couldn't see
the road in the day nor at night a star

I ate country eggs til the nests ran dry
and jalapeno peppers by the score
Like my stomach would be amused
to ask for more and more and more!

But more is a word that means naught to me!
Enough befits me more and more.
I wish I'd always felt this way
when someone knocked upon my door!

Though I haven't been able to travel the globe
The desire to do so ever present
Maybe God will let me see those places
like a harvest moon or a fishhook crescent

Enough befits me best, I'm sure.

THE BURDEN'S WE BEAR

It's not unusual to stumble beneath
The weight of a crumbling world
When the weight of the stars and bars
In a breeze is too much to unfurl!

It is not unusual to trip and fall
When running at the speed of light.
Even when I am scared to death,
I must face down more than fright.

It is not unusual to feel along
When we're running side by side
If we never take each other's hand
To help in being one another's guide

HAIKU FROM PAST AGES

The camera performs
A muted not while it is
Sitting on a shelf
A book does the same
It lies unread for more than a cook, quick, breath.
A pen and paper speak together words of love
In the pouring rain
They slept just beneath
Where sleeping dogs lie with pup
I took a picture
So, reflected
My gray in the new mirror
And thought, "God, I'm old!"

DARE I CHASE THE MYSTERY?

The romantic cry out for mystery,
The supernatural and the minstrelsy
It cries in the forest dark and cold
Pray for the dead and comfort the old.

It seeks not love, nor deadly war
Though by definition that's who we are
It seeks only peace in heart and soul
Neither white as snow nor black as coal!

The Romantic is Edgar Allen Poe
And Me... with pretty paper and bow
Knelt on one knee in fervent prayer
For the mystery of love I wouldn't dare

WHERE I RESIDE

I've had thoughts this day of Camelot,
Of King Author and the knightly Lancelot

I've had visions of the forest and the shire
Of mountain Dreams and Berried Desire!

I've seen Christmas trees and sugar plums
Dance together like fingers and thumbs.

I've watched the fire on the Christmas Day
And listened to carols along the way!

I've awakened to the joy of childish laughter
and awaited my chance to perfect hereafter!

I've longed for a journey upon the sea
and prayed for a lighthouse to welcome me!

I've waited and waited for dreams to come true
when they already had, when Only I knew

That my heart was a storehouse of places
And my mind a world of beautiful faces

Awaiting the words that would bring together
my sunshine dreams and stormy weather!

SEPTEMBER 18, 2020

Dragonflies and butterflies
Shadows flying through the air;
Mockingbirds and hummingbirds
Blue jays dropping on a dare

Red leaves are dancing on the wind
Pecans in clusters everywhere
Fall colors awaiting the fires of ever
Like pumpkins awaiting county fair

Mom bakes pies with aroma sweet
While children carve the faces there
Upon the front porch if memory serves
While rabbits seek a winder lair!

While harvest comes and seasons go,
and fields of cotton become more rare
I dream of days from my childhood
Sit on my front porch and go almost nowhere

THE INSPIRATIONALISTS

The wind and sun are in the east
Two cool and comfortable autumn beasts.

Where might Tracy turn out to be?
Interpreting someplace else? We'll see!

Or Kevin, who's counting on fingers and toes
To get my rhythm so, so, and so!

Where is Eilene with a comforting tear,
With the soul of a poet who's here to hear?

Where's Steve whose words are in tattoos
Or over the airway should he choose?

Where might Ron glean stories of woe
That travel form space to earth and grow

And who is this monster, this autumn beast
who pretends the most but gives the least?

A PERFECT DAY

Are we sure that it is Tuesday today?
It really seems more like a Sunday!

I have Celtic music on the stereo.
And a drastic need for some Ho! Ho! Ho!

The airs is as cool as a pumpkin's cry
Or a watermelon seep spit in my eye!

I can't wait to give thanks via poetry,
For that is the way God gave it to me.

A simple gift that through paper and pern
I'll be able to give again and again

Whether on Christmas morn with those I love
or with Jesus, God's greatest gift of love!

CHRISTMAS WISHES

I have had the strongest urge today to write
about autumn and winter and all of their
wonderful holidays!

I've prayed for rain and snow and cold,
Cold temperatures and room full of elves
 to decorate with no delays!

I have ribbons and bows and a thousand
good wishes to mail to family and
Friends by letters and cards.

Christmas trees, silverbells, and roaring
bonfires with carols and sleigh rides for
lonely forsaken old bards.

CHRISTMAS AT GRANDPA'S HOUSE

The dog sleeps close to the fireplace
as she would dare
Mama bakes sheets of sugar cookies
all with their usual care

The kids all pray for winter snow!
Red cheeks and chins are all aglow

Daddy comes inside from chopping wood
As only he and my grandaddy could

Mama adds a spoon of Pappy's molasses
to Daddy's coffee to thaw his glasses.

Mama's apron is near covered in flour
while the children await that magical hour

We were as poor a bunch as you might meet
But we didn't know it despite our cold feet;

For our socks had holes from heel to toe
In bread bag snow boots holes don't show

But Ma Turman would dry them over her stove
Then darn them to show her undying love

MICHAEL SHELTON

TALES OF PINE AND DELTA

Twenty-four of my relatives
died those years
Before Covid came to town:
That decade somewhere
between ninety-five
And an apocalyptic crown
As for me
I'll stay on top
Of the ground
Sing a version of the blues
with no renown
Neath the old magnolia tree
With my sweet southern belle!
Beneath the old magnolia tree
With my sweet southern belle
I'll sit and I'll swing
Mid the scent of the blooms
While I visit the past
Where I am bound with so many
 wonderful stories to tell!
Like two horses galloped
One black and one white
From the bright sunshine
Unto the depths of midnight
On All Hallows Eve
You drank a witch's brew
A toast to the moon
And to me and to you
As we passed the hours of one then two
And we galloped neath the moon riding two by two

While the pink carousel
Travelled around and around
While the black and the white
Whined not a sound
While the old magnolia
Whispered form the mound
"I have so many wonder stories to tell!"

MICHAEL SHELTON

THE DECK OF A SEAFARING MAN

Two orange pumpkins and maroon pompoms
Tootsie rolls, cokes and Trapp's dum dums

Pecans for the grownups for Christmas pies
Staying close to the kids like enemy spies

Watching out for demons who tell them lies
And real ghost stories about burgers and fries

Two old rockers from above and below
Sit stoically beside a globe full of snow

Lighthouses pray upon bended knew
To the God of hurricane lamps I see

While an old salt tells his tales of blues
And an albatross spreads her woeful news

I can no longer tell wedding guest from tar
Save one is a pumpkin and one is a star.

A PRAYER ON 10/15/2020

When in the depths of the woe and shame
I can call upon His Holy Name

For food or shelter, sick or lams;
To Him the answer is all the same;

For there is so little fortune and fame
Calls for a righteous biblical aim

That lots in church are naught but game
That sinners come to church to claim

And I am one with woe and shame
Who calls each day upon HIs name

To guide me forth within His Frame
Along the path, The Way I Came!

PERHAPS BLACK #19

Pecan fronds wave at me
Like a beauty queen waving
From the back of a new convertible
What you want are the fronds
The sky and convertible to be black
The Queen should be black
For the vengeance to be complete
Or perhaps I should be dead
In poverty grief stricken
Homeless depressed and sick uneducated
Mute blind and deaf
Perhaps I should have to appreciation
for the beauty of the queen
For poetry, art, God's handiwork,
my faith in him.
Perhaps I should stop helping
Stop giving, stop loving!
Don't know what color I am;
I've changed.

THE EWER #16

The ewer of tea is sweet, so sweet
The sun has steeped it
To a light golden brown
And warmed it into a throat soothing
Medicinal and herbal (???)
In it I can see solutions.
Through it I can see the unsolved.
Behind it I can see the power that made it.
Below it I can see the blue of Heaven.
Beneath it I can see the foundation
of bedrock and the future
With it, I can cue the ills
That man has created for himself
And by himself
But for now, it is but a muse
One creative muse
That tickles my otherwise stoic
Elbow and encourages it to smile.

ULTIMATE WISDOM

The rain will come sometime today
The trees have more than words to say

The squirrels and birds have their own way
To remind us to remember yesterday

For we've been taught to speak as one
Until that day when life is done

The spider's web will come undone
On the day its autumn race is won!

Walnuts pecans and peanut butter
feed my brain til it's all a flutter

Till fish and fowl stir silent rudder
and make me smart enough to mutter

Words that make me as wise as a tree
But never thinking once who might've made me!

THE KING OF SPRING

Bless the cardinal who sings of wealth
And the dove that coos for peace!
Bless the joys and bluebird's nest
And the warmth of the Shepard's fleece!

Gather ye birds of season all;
You are welcome in my home
As the elf, the owl, and birds of call,
The Leprechaun and the gnome!

In autumn I gather my winter stores
Whose lives sustain until spring
For birds for man thru mythical doors
While I sleep til hibernation's ring

When March arises with a roar
When man and beast together arise
I will sit upon my throne once more
Til the day the hue of autumn dies

FROSTY CHRISTMAS

It's freezing, frosty and silvery white!
I'll have to take a picture of it all tonight.

Meantime, I'll have to blow my nose
Wear layers and layers of winer clothes

Stay inside and drink warm, sweet tea
Hot chocolate and French Vanilla Coffee

This is my season my time of the year
To spread warm feelings, gifts, and cheer

So here is that gift, my virtual card
From a stark villain and Mantee bard

To my friends, family, everyone, I love
Merry Christmas, to all I'm thinking of!

BLUE TOES #10

Whew it's chilly, so chilly outside!
Wind is adding a frosty cold factor.
My memories are a hundred years wide,
Part time spent atop Pappy's tractor.

It was cold then, too… walking to the field
And leaving in a bale of cotton
It's warm all the way to the cotton gin
As this proved to be unforgotten

For the empty wagon is cold as snow
Ans so are my fingers and toes
Twenty little digits non-electronic
Turning bluer the further my Pappy goes

Now a field of briars is no laughing matter
Nor a second trip to the gin
Without my Granny's gravy and biscuit
Drippings off my little bare chin

SHE FED THEM THERE

She was borne by the wings
Of a lovesick arrow
Carried by kings and regal marrow!
They kept her imprisoned
In the deepest dungeon
Or starving in the highest tower,
A victim only a birth
And the most corrupted of power
She climbed onto the wicket gate
And over the garden wall
Across a beautiful snowcapped mount
Hidden in a youthful courtyard fount
Down a dark foreboding hall
Where wishes never die
And I'm never called upon to lie!
Bout the thousand who had she fed them there where
they were cherished.

MORNING! THEN AND NOW

A monarch a skipper and a bagworm cocoon
Let me know that winder will be soon
They will fight the wasps like a ten degree day
And rain leaves of red and yellow and gray

The sparrows are nesting in the wooden hayloft
The hay itself is comfortable and soft
The horses Winnie with a sad refrain
Or stand in the corral in the pouring rain

Butterflies of yellow black and gold
Await the fall harvest and late autumn colds
With bales of cotton on the way to the gin
And acres of corn filled one big bin

Pappy lets us ride til it's time for fishing
Or Mama Turman's kitchen sink is full of dishes
The field of sugar cane is ready for molasses
And for Pappy's collection of old snuff glasses!

WHEN ONCE I RACED A LION FOR LUNCH

A stir of cinnamon and sugar
With a tinge of caramel
My day begun with chocolate delight
and travelled the winder chapel bell.

With a taste of French Vanilla Café
And one of old Vienna
A drop of wine as red as blood
Or the rusty red of sienna.

My dragon has o'er slept the day
The dragon that is my muse!
What good a muse that tells a lie
And plays some unworthy ruse?

What good am I? No pen and Ink
With which to record my thoughts
Have I to comfort the raging river
And the loaves and fishes I've caught!

I spent the day in a flood of leaves
On a lake of sunshine and rain.
I traveled from one unto the other
Via my feelings and my brain

I shook my broken leg and heart
Till the middle of the afternoon
Stood erect and faced old Satan down
In the shadow of the evil moon!

As long as I can sit astride this world
And hold a meaningful position
I'll dig up war and plant my seed

To avoid any supposition!

I'll ship Fed Ex or UPS
And order by the same
When I have cash, I'll spend it
No matter how it's named!

MODERN POLITICS

No matter what the Donald does
Or if Biden can remember.
If Kamala is irrelevant
Or the queen comes back in December!
How many children can we kill
To get across our point?
How many bombs are set and blown
In the neighborhood bar or joint!

How many bridges and roads collapse?
How many mudslides or hurricanes?
How many fires via cigarettes can we ultimately claim?
Are we just shy of Heaven
Daily committing suicide
When does war and starvation become murderous homicide?

SOCIETY IN GENERAL

I have never ever owned a gun
But I own so many blades
How many people have been struck down
Behind closed curtains and shades

How many Covid, Ebola, and Aides
Can we count upon our fingers
How many naked pornographs
Are made today starring our children?

All is in the name of freedom of speech
Role models from sports and actors
Even politics is not exempt
Our heroes once drove tractors

Now the best of our soldiers are PTSD
Our policemen are angry and mistrusted
All of our children are ADD
And everybody's inappropriate or disgusted

A NEW START

There's a mockingbird pissed at all the cardinals
And seems to be winning the fight.
Is the name titmouses or titmice
I'm not sure just which one is right!
Although this seems a religious tract
Or a gospel song and dance
To say more would be no better right now
Then a simple little game of chance
After opening up my shoulder my bowels
My knee and my heart
And retiring from teaching I find myself
a poor misunderstood old bard
Who has many proteges and little food
To feed both stomach and soul,
But this little mind and damaged heart
With which to set new goals

RED AND YELLOW LEAVES

When I throw a dead leaf against the wind
Or against a raging storm
When I toss an apple into the air
or a cool and crispy morn

I know my autumn has arrived
with its bright blue harvest moon
It's colors of red and yellow times
That come each year eft soon!

Only its beauty in heaven will compare
And only its field on earth would dare
To put forth the colors of spring and fall
Brought forth in one autumnal call

The kirk of Scotland's Celtic gen
Resting a top the highlands
All were part of the Caledonians
And Canada's own newfoundland!

Is it any wonder I have found my home
Amide the Scottish and Irish gnome
Among the oaks and maple northeast
Or places I've yearned and longed to, see?

Is it any wonder I stand my ground
In any battle lost or treasure found
In the high lands or about the lowland glen
On the day of death in the Baskerville claw

Such has been this morning, this fall
With a scream from an eagle and a robin's call
On the ledge of kick or in its bell tower
Amid the chants of the priests with all their power

It's a journey unto Heaven on Angel's wings
Where a choir or nuns chant, dance or sing
In perfect rhythm and harmony
Of faith, hope, and eternal charity

DOG DUNG, SEWAGE, AND FIRE ANTS

Two stink and one hurts like hell
So, I stay upstairs with my cowbell

I write a line or three of poetry
When I'm not working on my biography

To afford retirement I sold my car
Medically I haven't been up to par

Then Covid came long and bailed me out
Who am I to fuss to say no and shout

So, I walk the front yard talk on the phone
Or go inside and watch reruns of "Bones"

Every now and then I read my bible
I love the New Testament of Christ disciples!

MISSISSIPPI

I love Mississippi and it's hospitality
Its music and all of its vocabulary

We talk to the animals like Dr. Doolittle
Politically we're stuck somewhere in the middle

For we give until it hurts and of ten times
We forgive those who wouldn't give us a dime

We love mother nature and sing her praises
We live by the Bible and quote its phrases

This is my Mississippi my life long home
Not Washington DC with its infamous dome

I'd rather sit on my deck
watch the birds at play
After I vote of course!
It's the American way!

DRESS BLUES

A sailor walked by in his navy blues
Reminding me of Daddy and last night news

For the day yesterday was election day
A loss so they say of the democratic way

Funny that I've lived for seventy years
Without losing my way nor a handful of tears!

No, we have thousands each day crying wolf
A generation of drunks with a head full of silt

I wanted to stop the sailor and shake his hand
Like my father had as a brother of the band!

His uniform stands as a symbol of peace
Like stories from Daddy that I cannot cease!

BLACK-EYED PEAS AND TURNIP GREENS

I went this summer
Back to my hometown
Though most of my kin folk were dead
And the young ones I had not met
It was a celebration of the black eyed pea
I wish it has been butterbeans!
Yes, it was the festival of the black eyed pea,
And I never ate a one;
Nobody had any mayo
That took out all the fun!
Miss Loudeen's Grocery is now a café
but the specialty is still a burger.
I wanted to order a push-up!
They offered me turnip greens
With a helping of rutabaga instead;
Hate them both when I was a kid
Haven't grown to like them as a man!
Not even country music helped
Nor Rhonda, my second grade love
Could take away the heartache.
From the hometown I once knew.
The candied yams are now in a can
The push-up a thing of the past
Nothing there at all where I once grew
Guess I knew it couldn't last!

WE ALL HAVE IT

Sing a song when you know that it's wrong
Take care of someone who is ill
Put your life ion the line
Swing merrily on the vine
And do it with consummate skill!

Do it without shame or embarrassment
No hesitation at all
Not for fame or compliment
A wrong, wrong number or call!
Don't let me fall
Don't le me waver or stall!

When we are in need
We can plant a seed
That comforts and feeds the world
Every boy and girl
With tresses and curls
Who're a victim of anger and greed!

EVEN GOD GOES TO STARKBUCKS

Instead of Starbucks I've gone to Chic-Fil-A
No other way than chicken my way!
Exercise follows when lattes are swallowed!
Eveready Bunny replaces the tallow!
Dead sea scrolls
And churches' rolls
Covenants from long, long past
Usurp the supporters repast!
Place down the blood of Christ
Offer up his body to vice!
Fill each heart with joy,
Come girl or boy
Offer gifts of eternal life
For, "I am the drum and the file"
Filled with life
Everlasting,
Everlasting life!

MISSISSIPPI RIVER

The river was low the captain hung over
When we reached the small hamlet of Dover

Dove was set in Louisiana upon a rise;
I built a lighthouse on the Mississippi side!

It never occurred to me that we'd run aground
On that fateful New Year's Eve
With all those bales of cotton aboard
And us bout to take our winter leave!

I owned both sides of the river bank
Stood many a day and night ashore
But I've never walked a single plank
Nor lost at poker when I kept score!

MICHAEL SHELTON

TWAS THE NIGHT BEFORE CHRISTMAS

The little old elf in his sooty red suit
Is missing a sock and a big black boot

He is eating cookies, a handful at a time
While I recorded his movements in rhythm and rhyme!

He slurps his milk that was warmed by the fire
And he counts each child and every desire

The smoke from his pipe rises in swirls
To match the one's wealth his cap and curls

He pulls on his socks, followed closely by boots
While he grunts and groans and hollers and hoots!

The mistletoe hung by a kiss and a thread
While the squirrels take pecans an acorns to bed

My what a Christmas already this year
Full of love thanksgiving music and cheer

THE DRAGON IN THE LIGHTHOUSE

MEET MICHAEL SHELTON

Living amid an airbase, an airport, and three air strips is nothing compared to a back yard filled with cardinals, mockingbirds, robins, crows, hawks, owls, wrens, (they're on my porch), and a few buzzards. At certain times of the year, we'd get geese and a few other migratory airborne rats and mice.

I'm used to country living, having been born and raised in Mantee, Mississippi with its less than two hundred population. Country church, country school, garden bicycle, bales of hay, and Pappy's sorghum molasses mill, sugar cane fields and farm animals. You can't get too much more country than that! There's plenty to write about!

Shade trees made good tree houses; pine made good igloos; uneven ground made great cone war bunkers. These were all of the elements that constitute my poetry.

My education was in Mississippi breeding at Elementary School in Cumberland, high school in West Point, and the rest of Mississippi State University. Work ethics came in factories, retail and the classroom, as a teacher.

With the scholarships and awards given me by poetry groups and educational outlet, I have had a life that is very close to perfect with the help of God, his perfect Son... and Mantee, Mississippi... My Eden. Twenty-five years of teaching has given me the rest. Hundreds of students have added what I couldn't, and I love them all for their contributions. I am truly blessed and hope to continue being so until my daughter and son agree to continue my legacy! LOL!

My Porch

My Back Yard

www.ingramcontent.com/pod-product-compliance
Lightning Source LLC
Chambersburg PA
CBHW051230120626
46547CB00013B/1590